Brown Girl Brown Girl

Written By Titilope O Ellis

Illustrated By Arsalan

This book belongs to _____

Copyright © 2022 By Titilope O Ellis

All rights reserved. No parts of this publication may be reproduced or transmitted in any form or by any means, mechanical or electronic to include photocopying and recording, without the prior written consent of the publisher, except in the case of brief quotations embodied in literary reviews.

Dedication

This book is dedicated to every brown girl in the world. There are no limits to the greatness that you can accomplish.

Brown girl
Brown girl,
what do you see?

Brown girl Brown girl, what do you see?

Brown girl
Brown girl,
what do you see?

Brown girl Brown girl, what do you see?

Brown girl Brown girl, what do you see?

Brown girl Brown girl, what do you see?

Brown girl Brown girl, do you love what you see?

Activity Time

Word Search

```
Z L M Q I S Y H L X L H B N H
B H C W N V I C T O R Y Y L E
H A E U T X A F A O S W I Y T
D W P J E R H R K V O U Y K A
B W S G L O S T R E N G T H Q
O X Z H L Y Z Y L R K U I B B
E E F S I A Q J D O I X H T N
C X U K G L T K G N V L D G F
G C X W E T Z D U P V E O X J
P E E A N Y Y Z O G K Y A W O
U Q D X C D G I J R R E J Y Y
L W K L E X C E V Q H F E E E
U F C O U R A G E D I E D M M
V G D U G Y K U W O E G Y W N
E U Q M S G M C N C H X X J F
```

Intelligence   Strength   Courage   Love
Victory   Royalty   Joy

Reflection Time

1) What does courage mean to you? Give an example of a time you showed courage.

2) What does intelligence mean to you? Give an example of a time you felt intelligent.

3) What does joy mean to you? Give an example of a time you felt joyful.

4) What does royalty mean to you? Give an example of a time you felt royal?

5) What does strength mean to you? Give an example of a time you used your strength.

6) What does victory mean to you? Give an example of a time you felt victorious

7) What does love mean to you? Name all the people and things you love (hint, don't forget to include yourself).

CPSIA information can be obtained
at www.ICGtesting.com
Printed in the USA
BVHW011055220223
658989BV00018B/485